CURRENCY MINI DRAMAS

Daniel Evans

OPENING A FUZZWOLLOP'S FRAME OF MIND

CURRENCY PRESS, SYDNEY

CURRENCY MINI DRAMAS

First published in 2002
by Currency Press Pty Ltd,
PO Box 2287, Strawberry Hills, NSW, 2012, Australia
enquiries@currency.com.au
www.currency.com.au

Reprinted 2015, 2017, 2018, 2019, 2020, 2022

Cataloguing-in-publication data for this title is available
from the National Library of Australia website:
www. nla.gov.au

Publication of this title was assisted by the
Commonwealth Government through the Australia
Council, its arts funding and advisory body.

Set by Dean Nottle.
Cover design by Kate Florance.
Printed by Fineline Print + Copy Services, Revesby, NSW.

Opening a Fuzzwollop's Frame of Mind was first produced by Synergy Theatre Company at the Brisbane Arts Theatre, as part of the Brisbane Festival of Arts, on 26 August 2001, with the following cast:

Judith	Michelle Giufre
Jethro	Daniel Evans
Wilmah	Maranne McQuade
Zilpah	Chiara Hesse
Eyre	Natalie Giufre
Anon	Karleigh Bauer
Magnus	Marissa Martin

Director, Anthea Lock
Producer, Katrina Torenbeek

Characters

Eyre, the new being whose innocence often leads to conflict and an awakening of harsh truth

Wilmah, an endearing old soul who has misplaced her life's purpose and, worse yet, forgotten its name

Zilpah, a cynical bookworm whose love for all things textual is bordering on disturbing

Judith Hartwig, an upper-class elitist whose extravagant amount of jewellery is surpassed only by her extravagant ego

Jethro Hartwig, a conceited sophisticate who is loyal to his wants, his wine and dollar signs

Anon, a young and mysterious artist whose paintings hold an intriguing story, if only he could talk

Magnus, a burly woman whose dark presence casts a shadow over the room

Setting

A room with two black windows and one black door. A fluorescent light is suspended above the stage and is in the audience's view.

This play is dedicated to all those who hold the key. May you find its purpose and have the courage to use it.

From somewhere behind the curtain an old scratchy record begins to play 'The Blue Danube'. The music gradually grows louder. Suddenly the curtains part; Mrs Judith Hartwig and Mr Jethro Hartwig enter waltzing. The music dies down.

Judith [*sullenly*] Jethro, darling, do you sometimes wonder what it would have been like if we had—?

Jethro [*interrupting*] Yes.

Judith Tell me again, why didn't we?

Jethro It was the unknown.

Judith Ah, the unfamiliar.

Jethro The unascertained.

Judith The undiscovered.

Jethro The unexplored.

Judith The uninvestigated.

Jethro The unrevealed.

Judith The un… un…

Jethro [*whispering in her ear*] Unearthed.

Judith Oh, thank you, darling. The unearthed.

They waltz a while.

Jethro The fact was we were—

Judith Don't say!

Jethro Scared.

Judith Frightened.

Jethro Alarmed.

Judith Worried.

Jethro Unsure.

Judith Terrified.

Jethro Apprehensive.

Judith We were... ah... oh...

Jethro [*whispering in her ear*] Afraid.

Judith Oh, thank you, darling. Afraid.

Jethro But we're comfortable, are we not?

Judith Why, yes. Yes! I suppose so.

Jethro And we're happy?

Judith [*uncertain*] Actually, now that I consider it...

Jethro No?

Judith No.

Jethro No? So you are happy.

Judith No. 'No' as in 'no, I'm not happy'.

Jethro Well, why don't you look at your jewellery.

Judith I... I... I don't think that's going to make me happy anymore.

She suddenly stops waltzing.

She made me realise that money can't buy certain things. Yes, it can buy sapphire rings and ruby necklaces but it can't buy…

Jethro Diamonds?

Judith [*longingly*] Freedom.

Jethro The ability to fly like a bird.

Judith Soar like an eagle.

Jethro To come down from the bleachers and onto the field.

Judith To… to…

Jethro [*whispering in her ear*] To cut the—

Judith Jethro, please, give me a chance! [*She pauses. Solemnly*] To walk out of the door.

> *The music strikes up again as Jethro takes Judith in his arms and begins to waltz again. Judith gazes longingly somewhere else. The curtains part as they spin in an exit.*
>
> *The music is brought to a halt by a high-pitched scream from Judith. There is the sound of many people rushing. Silence. The curtains open to reveal a clump of people encircling something.*

Wilmah What on Jupiter is it?

Jethro How did it get here?

Judith For goodness sakes, Jethro! We know how it got here!

Jethro How, darling?

Judith I was sitting over there, minding my own jewellery when…

Wilmah When?

Jethro When?

Wilmah When, what?

Jethro Yes, darling, when what?

Judith [*confused*] What?

Wilmah Yes, what?

Jethro Yes, darling, what?

Judith What, when this thing appeared before my very eyes! It was as though it appeared out of thin air.

Jethro As though it came from nowhere.

Judith As though it suddenly became visible.

Jethro As though it raised and became evident.

Judith As though… as though…

Jethro [*whispering in her ear*] As though it came into being.

Judith Why, thank you, darling. As though it came into being.

Wilmah Yes, but what exactly is it?

They all look to Zilpah, who breaks off from the encirclement and reaches for one of his books. He skims through it until he finds his page.

4

Zilpah It has all the obligatory qualities along with the organic neurons of being a…

Judith A goat?

Jethro An alien?

Wilmah A Fuzzwollop?

Judith A Fuzzwopwop?

Jethro A Fuzzwolla?

Wilmah No, a Fuzzwollop.

Judith It couldn't be that!

Jethro No, it couldn't!

Judith Frankly said, there is no way it could.

Wilmah Who let Frankly decide?

Jethro Frankly?

Judith Who is Frankly?

Wilmah You just said Frankly said!

Jethro I don't know a Frankly!

Judith Well, of course you wouldn't, Jethro. We do not socialise with the Franklys.

Jethro We don't?

Judith No.

Jethro Oh.

Judith They're of…

Jethro Of what?

Judith You know…

Jethro No, I don't know.

Judith The Franklys are of the lower class.

Jethro I see.

Wilmah But you just said, 'Fredly said, "Snails taste like chicken".'

Judith Snails?

Jethro Chicken?

Zilpah [*in a fit of rage*] Human!

Judith Zilpah, so you've tasted them?

Jethro And they taste like us?

Zilpah No, the thing is a…

Wilmah Fuzzwollop. Frankly said so.

Zilpah [*extremely aggravated*] No! It's a human!

> *Magnus, who hasn't been watching, turns curiously. Anon perks his head up from where he is drawing. Judith and Jethro have a wave of disappointment upon them. Wilmah laughs. They all stare at her.*

Wilmah [*through a fit of giggles*] Well, I told you it was a Fuzzwollop.

Judith Wilmah, it's a human.

Jethro A human being.

Judith Just another one of us.

Jethro Just another—

Wilmah Fuzzwollop! A Fuzzwollop is exactly that—a human.

Judith I must say that was rather disappointing.

Jethro I must say I agree with you, darling.

Judith It could have been a goat but, oh no, it had to be a human.

Jethro A mortal.

Judith A bipedal.

Jethro One of us.

Judith A… an… one… oh!

Jethro [*whispering in her ear*] A Fuzzwollop.

Judith Thank you, darling. A Fuzzwollop.

Wilmah [*thinking aloud*] No, it's more like beef.

Jethro Pardon?

Wilmah Snails, they taste like beef.

Judith Who said so?

Wilmah Fredly.

Jethro Oh, Fredly. He must be the one that we choose not to socialise with.

Judith Darling, that's Frankly. Fredly is that kind horse jockey who gave me my emerald signature ring. See, there it is.

She indicates one of her rings.

My… wasn't that a long time ago? [*She pauses.*] Anyway, Fredly wouldn't have said that snails taste like chicken.

Jethro Then who did?

Wilmah [*looking up at Jethro*] It was… It!

Jethro I will not be referred to as a pronoun.

Wilmah I never said you were an ant mound.

Judith I swear, Jethro, [*pointing to Wilmah*] she is batty!

Jethro Well, darling, that is old news! Who is It?

Judith It, what?

Jethro It. Wilmah called me It!

Judith But what did It do?

Jethro It ate snails.

Judith Snails?

Jethro Yes.

Judith And were they crunchy?

Jethro How should I know?

Judith Well, you ate them, darling!

Jethro I did nothing of the sort!

Judith Then who ate snails?

Wilmah It did!

Judith Who is It?

Wilmah It is that!

She points to Eyre.

Judith I see, so It ate snails and It said they tasted like chicken.

Wilmah Did It really do that?

Judith Well, you just said… That's it!

Wilmah Well, I know that's It. We've met.

Judith No, I mean… Honestly, Jethro, it's like talking to a cement wall.

Jethro No, darling, it's a brick wall.

Judith Don't you start!

Judith and Jethro storm furiously to the back and sit down. They have a mute conversation, though it is clear they're discussing Wilmah. Magnus picks up some knitting needles and begins to knit. Anon, who has been smiling throughout their argument, studies Eyre and begins to sketch her. Zilpah continues to read. Wilmah walks up to Eyre and kneels beside her. She studies her for a while. Eyre's vocabulary is very simple and her speech isn't yet developed completely.

Eyre Hello.

Wilmah So you can talk!

There is a pause.

Do they taste like chicken or beef?

Eyre I do not understand.

Wilmah Snails? Do they taste like chicken or beef?

Eyre I have not met a snail, so I would not know.

Wilmah [*confused*] But you're It! You're supposed to know!

Eyre No…

Wilmah No?

Eyre Not It, I'm—

Wilmah That, who, which, what, his, her, yours, you?

Eyre Eyre.

Wilmah Well, yes dear, it's all around you. Just breathe in.

Eyre No, my name Eyre. What your name?

Wilmah Wilmah Wilfred Wendell. Pleased to meet you, Eyre. So who are you?

Eyre I am Eyre.

Wilmah Well, yes, I know you're Eyre, dear, but why are you here?

Eyre [*confused*] I do not understand.

Wilmah I see. [*Very slowly*] Why are you [*pointing to her*] here?

Eyre [*copying her dispatch*] I do not understand.

Wilmah Well, dear, what is your purpose?

Eyre [*struggling with the correct pronunciation*] Purrr… purrp… purpose.

Wilmah Not porpoise, dear. Purpose.

Eyre [*pronouncing with relative ease*] Purpose?

Wilmah Yes, dear, what is your purpose?

Eyre What is purpose?

Wilmah Well, dear, your purpose is your reason for living. You see, bees collect pollen to make honey, that is their purpose, and teddy bears make people—

Eyre Bees? What are they?

Wilmah Bees are… oh dear, I'm afraid I'm not explaining this right.

Eyre What is right?

Wilmah Right is the opposite of wrong.

Eyre What is wrong?

Wilmah Wrong is… wrong is the… ah…

Unable to explain she turns to Eyre.

Eyre Wilmah, what your purpose?

Wilmah [*excited*] Well, my purpose is to be a… a…

Judith [*yelling from the back*] A blithering idiot!

Wilmah [*saddened*] I don't know. I don't have a purpose. I guess I'm purposeless.

Eyre How do you find purpose?

Wilmah I'm… I'm not quite sure. I think… I think you need to call it.

She rises to her feet.

[*Calling*] Purpose! Purpose! Are you here? Mummy is getting very mad! Purpose! Purpose!

Eyre Maybe, you need to call name. My name Eyre. Your name Wilmah. Purpose name…

Wilmah Oh yes, that's it, dear! His name is Alvin! Alvin! Oh, Alvin? Wait, no that wasn't his name. Now, what was it? Hector? No. Wyzegeyser? No. Vendetta? No. [*She pauses a while to think.*] Fuvzat! That was my purpose's name. Fuvzat! Fuvzat! [*Shouting*] Fuvzat! For the love of McNutty, I almost forgot, he's very small.

She drops to her knees and begins to crawl around the stage.

[*Whispering*] Fuvzat. Fuvzat.

Eyre stays where she is and begins to call quietly.

Eyre Fuvzat. Fuvzat.

Wilmah stops crawling and looks horrified at Eyre.

Wilmah Oh, dear, you aren't very smart, are you?

Eyre Smart? What is smart?

Wilmah Well, dear, being smart is the act of thinking and being intelligent.

Eyre [*confused*] Why me not smart?

Wilmah Fuvzat was sitting there just a few moments ago. You're sitting on him, dear. Oh, my poor Fuvzat. [*She bursts into tears.*] Oh, Fuvzat, he's gone. My little purpose is gone. He was a good purpose you know. Oh, but now… now… he's gone.

> *Eyre rises from the ground for the first time and tries to walk. She stands, stumbles and falls. This is repeated until she finally can stand and walk. She examines the spot where she was sitting. Wilmah continues to wail.*

Oh, he's gone. Oh, what am I going to do? Where am I going to find another purpose? Oh, Fuvzat he's… he's…

Eyre He not here, Wilmah.

Wilmah [*through tears*] I know that, dear! Do you really need to rub it in? Oh, Fuvzat!

Eyre I not sitting on him.

> *Wilmah suddenly stops wailing and looks very shocked.*

Wilmah What?

Eyre He not here.

Wilmah What did you say?

Eyre When?

Wilmah Before when, dear.

Eyre I said, he not here.

Wilmah Are you sure, dear?

Eyre Well, I got up from ground and I not see Fuvzat anywhere.

Wilmah So you mean to say, there is still hope for my purpose?

Eyre Hope?

Wilmah Is there?

Eyre What is hope?

Wilmah Hope is the act of believing, dear.

Eyre Believing, what?

Wilmah [*excited*] That we may be in with a chance!

Eyre What, chance?

Wilmah The chance that my Fuvzat might still be alive!

She claps her hands together in sheer joy and looks up at Eyre.

Well, come on dear, we have to start looking!

Eyre kneels to the ground with Wilmah.

We will have to be very quiet. [*Whispering*] My Fuvzat gets very overwhelmed by loud noise. Fuvzat! Fuvzat! Come out, come out, wherever you are! Fuvzat! Fuvzat!

Eyre [*calling quietly*] Fuvzat! Fuvzat!

Wilmah Oh my!

Eyre What?

Wilmah Well, I almost forgot, we have to look for your purpose too! Now what is his name?

Eyre I not know.

Wilmah Inotknow? Now that *is* an odd name! Nevertheless we can kill two stones with one bird. You call Inotknow and I'll call Fuvzat. Fuvzat! Fuvzat!

Eyre No. I mean, I do not know.

Wilmah Well, dear, make up your mind! Is it Inotknow or Idonotknow?

Eyre I do not know my purpose's name.

Wilmah Dear, you could've just said that! Now, let's try and think of your purpose's name. Is it Charlie?

Eyre No.

Wilmah Is it Nelson?

Eyre No, I don't think so.

Wilmah Is it Eugene?

Eyre No.

Wilmah Is it Luther, dear?

Eyre No.

Wilmah Is it—?

Eyre Wait. Luther! That my purpose name. Luther!

Wilmah Well, dear, now we can start looking! Fuvzat! Fuvzat! Fuvzat! Oh, where are you?

> *Wilmah crawls around the stage silently calling for her purpose. Eyre begins to crawl over to Zilpah calling for her purpose. She accidentally bangs her head on one of the many piles of Zilpah's books, sending it toppling. An enraged Zilpah stands up and hovers above her.*

Zilpah Who are you?

Eyre Who are you?

Zilpah I asked you first.

Eyre I am Eyre.

Zilpah Oh, so you're the new one. [*Inspecting her*] Interesting specimen, aren't you? An ordinary human being with the standard thorax, cranium and spine. Yet your speech is somewhat under-developed. Perhaps you are dull.

Eyre What is dull?

Zilpah Dull, my dear lady, is an adjective. It means stupid.

Eyre What is stupid?

Zilpah My, you really are stupid.

Eyre How I be stupid, if I know not what it means?

Zilpah Quite an interesting philosophy, I must write it down.

>*He reaches for a book and begins to scribble furiously in it.*

Eyre Who are *you*?

Zilpah [*astounded*] Who am I? Who am I? I am Zilpah the Magnificent! Known right across the room I am! I am the answer to all questions. I am the silent brain behind all master plots. I am spilling over with knowledge.

Eyre What is knowledge?

Zilpah Knowledge is a noun, it means being well-informed and having the utmost experience in any given matter.

Eyre How do you experience knowledge?

Zilpah By reading, studying, revising and referring to books.

Eyre What book?

Zilpah A book is what you politely collided into just a few moments ago. I must say that was very imprudent, you interrupted my study of computing without nerve impulses. I was into the pivotal part of the exploration of the non-spiking neurons, which can be strangely observed in a lobster's stomach.

Eyre What book used for?

Zilpah To gain a wealth of desirable knowledge. For, you see, knowledge is the key to living, for if you don't have knowledge then what do you have?

Eyre I not know.

Zilpah You have a carcass.

Eyre What do with knowledge?

Zilpah [*pointing to his head*] You store it up here.

Eyre How does it fit?

Zilpah No, you don't store it in your head, you store it in your brain.

Eyre What is brain?

Zilpah A brain is the nervous matter in your skull, your intellect.

Eyre What do once knowledge in brain?

Zilpah You keep it there in case.

Eyre Incase, what?

Zilpah Incase, you need to apply it to a situation.

Eyre What for?

Zilpah To do good.

Eyre You use often?

Zilpah Yes. Well, no. No, most of the time I am reading, studying, revising and then referring.

Eyre What for?

Zilpah To gain knowledge.

Eyre What do with knowledge?

Zilpah I've already told you, I apply it to do good.

Eyre Do you apply often?

Zilpah Yes. Well, no. Most of the time I am reading, studying, revising and then referring.

Eyre What for?

Zilpah [*becoming aggravated*] To gain knowledge.

Eyre What do you do with knowledge?

Zilpah I apply it!

Eyre Do you apply often?

Zilpah Yes. Well, no. No, I don't. Most of the time I have my head stuck in a book memorising a whole bunch of useless facts that I only use once in a lifetime. There, are you quite happy now? I have nothing to apply my knowledge to! Except trivial matters which, being downright honest, are a complete waste of time and don't even require me to exercise my brain!

Eyre You are strange.

Zilpah Well, there you go. A new title already. Zilpah the Strange! Now, can you please go away. I wish to wallow in my self-pity. [*Talking aloud to himself*] All those years of cramming knowledge and what for? Nothing. Only to be told by some stupid new bipedal that— [*Noticing Eyre*] What do you want?

Eyre I just wondering… Well, I wanted to… [*Spitting it out*] Have you seen Luther?

Zilpah Who is Luther?

Eyre My purpose.

Zilpah Your purpose has a name?

Eyre Yes.

Zilpah Well, I hate to be the one to tell you this but, [*with contempt*] purposes don't come with a nametag. They are a quality which resides within you. A purpose is an intention, a design, an aim, an object or result which is strived for. It is there but it isn't. It won't come with the call of a name, you have to discover it. So there is no use calling Luper because it won't work.

Eyre His name is Luther. [*Calmly*] Do books tell you?

Zilpah [*sourly*] Do books tell me what?

Eyre Purpose have no name?

Zilpah No. It's commonsense.

Eyre Commonsense?

Zilpah It's just standard knowledge. Nobody in his or her right mind would crawl around calling for something that isn't there.

Wilmah [*calling quietly*] Fuvzat! Fuvzat! No luck here, any luck with locating Luther?

Zilpah My point exactly.

Eyre Luther not found yet.

Wilmah Well, I shall keep looking. I won't rest until Fuvzat has been found.

Eyre I rest not as well.

Wilmah Together we will find our purposes. Now, Eyre, you look up there near Mr and Mrs Hart*pig*.

> *She laughs to herself.*
> *Eyre crawls, making her way beneath the table of Judith and Jethro. She clambers about. Judith and Jethro, who are unaware of what is happening, arouse and begin talking. Eyre accidentally squashes Judith's toe.*

Judith [*painfully*] Ouch! Jethro, what did you do that for?

Jethro [*inquiring*] Do what, darling?

Judith You just stamped on my foot.

Jethro Sorry, darling, I don't recall touching your foot at all.

Judith [*spitefully*] Well, darling, as long as you didn't mean to do it. Then I will have to forgive you, won't I?

Judith gives Jethro a harsh look before turning her head away. Eyre accidentally treads on her foot again.

[*Through gritted teeth*] Ouch! Jethro, would you please stop that!

Jethro Stop what?

Judith Stop that.

Jethro Stop what?

Judith Stop doing what you're doing!

Jethro But I'm not doing anything?

Judith [*enraged*] Oh, yes you are.

Jethro Oh, no I'm not.

Judith You stood on my foot.

Jethro I did no such thing.

Judith Then who did?

Jethro You did!

Judith Jethro, I am a woman of sophistication. I am not an imbecile who kicks feet!

Jethro I'm telling you, darling, I did not step on your foot!

Judith glares at Jethro. Eyre accidentally treads on Jethro's foot.

Ow! What was that for?

Judith What was what for?

Jethro You stood on my foot.

Judith I did not.

Jethro [*childish*] Did too!

Judith [*childish*] Did not!

Jethro Did too!

Judith Did not!

Jethro Did too!

Judith Did not!

Jethro Did too!

Judith intends to kick Jethro but instead kicks Eyre.

Judith [*savagely*] Take that!

Jethro Take what?

Judith I just kicked you.

Jethro No, you did not.

Judith I did! Did you not feel it?

Jethro I felt nothing.

Judith You're cheating!

Jethro Cheating?

Judith Yes, that is correct, you are cheating.

Jethro What?

Judith I must say it is completely understandable.

Jethro [*bewildered*] Have you gone mad?

Judith I bet you are wearing shin pads.

Jethro Shin pads?

Judith Yes, shin pads.

Jethro I am not.

Judith [*judiciously*] Well, there is only one way to find out.

> *Judith peers under the table. Eyre stares at her. Judith takes one look at her and re-appears above the table.*

[*Shrieking*] Jethro! Jethro!

Jethro So I was wearing shin pads? Yes, I cheated! I admit it! It is the only way to win with you, Judith! I decided that I would wear shin pads just in case you decided—

Judith Shut up, Jethro! That thing is under there!

Jethro Thing?

Judith Yes, the thing!

Jethro What thing?

Judith The thing that appeared before my very eyes!

Jethro Oh, *that* thing! And it's where?

Judith Beneath the table!

Jethro Why?

Judith I don't know, darling, but get it out!

Jethro How?

Judith Jethro, must I do all the thinking around here? [*Sighing*] Push, shove and use tongs if you have to! Just get the thing out!

> *Jethro puts his head beneath the table. Eyre looks puzzled, dazed and sad. Judith appears panicked.*

Jethro [*politely introducing himself*] Hello. I am Jethro Hartwig, wife of Judith Hartwig. Would you mind coming above our table?

Judith No, Jethro, not up here! It might have a disease! It may want to steal my jewellery!

Jethro Settle down, Judith. It is only young. [*Greeting Eyre with a smile*] What do you say? Would you like to come up? It is rather cold down here. Come on.

> *Jethro reappears above the table. Eyre surfaces above the table. Judith cowers away from Eyre.*

Judith Jethro, darling, please dispose of it!

Eyre I have name.

Jethro See, Judith, it isn't completely uncivilised! It has a name.

Eyre Uncivilised?

Judith My, isn't she young?

Jethro Innocent.

Judith Virtuous.

Jethro Young.

Judith Youthful.

Jethro Inexperienced.

Judith Waiting to bloom.

Jethro Waiting to awaken.

Judith Waiting to flourish.

Jethro Waiting to prosper.

Judith Waiting… waiting… oh…

Jethro [*whispering in her ear*] Waiting to be taught.

Judith Thank you, darling. Waiting to be taught. [*Excited*] Taught! Oh, darling, I will be its teacher and it will be my pupil.

Eyre My name not It. My name Eyre.

Judith Oh, whatever, darling. Now…

Eyre [*bewildered*] My name Eyre.

Judith Oh, Jethro, the thing wants to exchange names with me! How exciting! So, Eyre, what is your surname?

Eyre Surname?

Judith Your surname is your last name. My last name is Hartwig. So…

Eyre Hartwig? [*Confused*] Not Hartpig?

Judith [*with disgust*] Hartpig? Who told you my surname was Hartpig?

Eyre Wilmah.

Judith Oh, her! Well, that doesn't surprise me at all. She is a menace to society!

Eyre Society?

Judith Why, do not tell me you know nothing about the lower society, middle society or high society.

Eyre No, nothing.

Judith Well, the lower society has no manners and takes no pride in their outer appearance. They have no money or possessions. The absence of these qualities is what separates them from the middle society. The middle society has mild manners and takes average concern in their outer cleanliness and appearance. They have enough money and typical possessions. Are you following this?

Eyre nods.

However, the high society has the utmost care and pride in their appearance. They are always dressed properly and they have not one inch of dirt to be found upon them. They have an abundance of money, which buys them notable possessions, and beautiful decorations to improve and reflect their appearance.

Eyre Who in which class?

Judith What an intelligent question! [*Half to herself*] She really is a dingbat. [*To Eyre, full of smiles*] Well, Wilmah is in the lower society because of her quirky traits and ugly outer appearance. Zilpah can be classed as the middle society because of his mild manners, which are fine in small doses. Although his outward appearance needs work. His possessions are average but they don't hold enough value to separate him from the middle and high society.

Eyre Who is in the high society?

Judith That's right, your grammar is getting better. The high society is Jethro and I. You see we take care in looking after our appearance, we are lavishly decorated with jewellery and we have notable possessions. We have an abundance of money and, put plainly, money makes the world go around.

Eyre Me belong to what society?

Judith Well, which society do you wish to belong to?

Eyre High?

Judith Well, if you wish to belong to our society, we shall have to clean you up.

She inspects Eyre's face.

Your eyes are bright, your eyelashes are long and curled, but your cheeks appear to be tear-streaked. Have you been crying?

Eyre Crying?

Judith I am dreadfully sorry, I forgot you are only new to this world. Have you had water come out of your eyes?

Eyre I think so.

Judith When?

Eyre When I was under the table looking for Luther. I felt something hard kick into me…

Judith [*with guilt*] I am sure that was Jethro.

Jethro [*shocked*] Me! As I recall it was you!

Judith Me! You were the one doing all the kicking!

Jethro I don't think so!

Judith Jethro, it was you!

Jethro Me?

Judith Yes.

Jethro No, it was not!

Judith Yes, it was!

Jethro No, it was not!

Judith Yes, it was!

Jethro [*childish*] Was not!

Judith [*childish*] Was too!

Jethro Was not!

Judith Was too!

> *Eyre rises and leaves. Judith and Jethro continue to bicker, but their words become mute as Eyre approaches Anon.*

Eyre Hello.

> *Anon continues to draw a picture.*

Hello. My name Eyre.

> *Anon ignores her and continues to draw a picture.*

Hello. My name Eyre. What is your name?

Wilmah [*crawling forward*] Fuvzat. Fuvzat. [*She notices Eyre. Giggling*] He can't hear you. He lives in a world of his own. Anon is his name. We call him that; it's short for Anonymous. He prefers not to be known. He never speaks, you know, the tiger has his tongue.

Eyre Oh.

Wilmah Any luck finding Luther?

Eyre No. Mr and Mrs Hartwig didn't offer any help.

Wilmah I didn't think they would. Still, we've got to keep looking! We can't give up yet.

Wilmah crawls away calling for her purpose. Eyre is about to crawl away when she glances at the picture Anon is drawing and stops still.

Eyre What is that?

Anon [*whispering*] A picture.

Eyre You talk.

Anon A picture.

Eyre That picture it looks…

Anon Like you have seen it.

Eyre Yes. What is it of?

Anon I draw a lot of pictures.

Eyre What are they about?

Anon Places.

Eyre Do you draw places that you make up in your brain?

Anon Places.

Eyre Do you draw places that are in this room?

Anon Places.

Eyre Places that are… outside of this room?

Anon continues to draw. Magnus perks her head up and stares at Eyre.

Eyre Anon? Do you draw places that are— ?

Magnus [*interrupting*] Child, do not talk to him. He cannot hear you.

Eyre He can! He talking to me about how he draws places that is—

Magnus Child, come here!

> *Eyre walks to Magnus who is staring intently at her.*

Eyre [*frightened*] Who are you?

Magnus I am Magnus, I control this room. I make sure it remains comfortable.

Eyre My name is—

Magnus Eyre. I have heard. You are looking for your purpose called Luther.

Eyre How—?

Magnus How did I know? It is my duty as the master to know everything that goes on in this room. I suppose you do not know what a room is?

Eyre I have heard about it.

Magnus A room is a place where people can live happily and comfortably. It normally consists of at least one window—

Eyre Window?

Magnus [*pointing to a window*] One of those things.

Eyre Why is it black?

Magnus To stop the outside getting in.

Eyre The outside. That is what Anon's pictures are about.

Magnus I see you are gaining a comprehension. Do not pay any attention to his pictures. They are a complete waste of time and space.

Eyre They beautiful.

Magnus Tell me, Eyre, are you comfortable?

Eyre Yes.

Magnus Are you happy?

Eyre I think so.

Magnus Then why do you want to look at the outside? If you are happy and comfortable here.

Eyre I don't know.

Magnus Then continue looking for your purpose in here, where you are happy and comfortable and think not of the outside again.

Eyre [*dazed*] Yes.

Magnus continues to knit but stops again.

Magnus Child, do not mention our little chat to anybody.

Eyre turns and drops to the floor. Wilmah crawls up beside her. Eyre turns to her and whispers.

Eyre Any luck?

Wilmah Nope. You?

Eyre No. Wilmah?

Wilmah Yes, dear.

Eyre Can I tell you something?

Wilmah Of course, dear.

Eyre Promise not to tell, especially Magnus.

Wilmah My lips are walrused.

Eyre I thinking.

Wilmah Thinking?

Eyre Yes.

Wilmah About what?

Eyre About… [*very quietly*] outside.

Wilmah [*shouting*] You've been thinking about the outside!

Judith [*turning from bickering*] Thinking about what?

Jethro What is what?

Zilpah About…

Wilmah With reference to…

Judith In regard to…

Jethro What?

Zilpah The outside.

Wilmah [*drawing a deep breath*] He said it!

Judith Out aloud.

Jethro In public.

Judith It's unbelievable.

Jethro Treacherous.

Judith Treasonable.

Jethro Illegal.

Judith Prohibited.

Jethro Forbidden.

Judith Banned.

Jethro He's been bootlegging.

Judith He's been… been… oh!

Jethro [*whispering in her ear*] He's been thinking depravity.

Judith Thank you, darling. He's been thinking depravity.

Wilmah Timbers me shiver. I would never have thought you were capable of it, Zilpah. Dear heart, you were always such a nice man. Filled with promise and knowledge. He always looked comfortable and happy but now we know. He was simply putting on a facade. You know, I had always suspected something wasn't entirely right with Zilpah ever since he began reading more and more and more and more and more of those books. He seemed to separate himself from human kind much like an ant. You try to make friends with an ant and they just crawl away. Ants are very hostile creatures, you know. Did you know one bit me? I was only trying to shake his hand and… and… what on Jupiter am I talking about?

Zilpah [*shouting*] I don't know, you silly old fool! For your information, Mr and Mrs High and Mighty, [*referring to Judith and Jethro*] it wasn't me who was thinking outside the room. It was her! Her! Not me! And you wonder why I separate myself from you lot. It's because you are insane. Yes, you heard me, insane! You make a mountain out of a molehill. You—

Wilmah [*giggling*] Mountain out of a molehill? Have you ever heard of such idiocy? Dear, dear, how did you figure that?

Zilpah Wilmah! It's a colloquialism! An expression! It isn't supposed to reflect reality! What I was saying is, I can find more friends in knowledge and books than I will ever find here!

Judith Now you listen here, Zilpah. How dare you accuse Eyre of thinking… well, you know… outside the room. She is a woman of high society and women of high society do not let their thoughts stray outside of their beauty and possessions.

Jethro My wife is right, Eyre would never do that! She is young and innocent! How dare you implicate that she has been thinking outside! A man of your knowledge should know better!

36

Eyre [*standing up weakly*] No. I was thinking outside.

Judith Well, I never…

Jethro Good grief!

Eyre When I first arrived here, I was lonely. In short time, I have befriended by most… all of you! Wilmah taught me that everybody has a purpose and though I may have lost it, she would help me look. Zilpah taught me knowledge could help people and purpose can't be called by a name. Mr and Mrs Hartwig helped—

Zilpah Where is all this leading?

Eyre [*continuing on*] Most important lesson I learnt came from Anon who taught me there is more than just this room. I want to tell you this. We don't have to stay in here. We can go outside.

Zilpah See! I told you she said it!

Judith She said it, darling!

Jethro She did!

Wilmah Outside.

Zilpah Outside.

Judith Outside.

Jethro Outside.

Zilpah Theoretically speaking there is no way of leaving these four walls.

Judith No escape.

Jethro No exit.

Judith No departure.

Jethro No migration.

Judith No fleeing.

Jethro No exiting.

Judith No… no… oh!

Jethro [*whispering to her*] No hope.

Judith Why, thank you, darling! No hope!

Eyre That isn't true. We could climb out a window.

Judith Window! Who ever heard of anything so ludicrous?

Jethro Window? I don't believe I've met him before.

Judith Oh, of course you have, darling. He was my mother's lawyer.

Jethro Oh, that Window. He was a nice chap.

Judith Yes, he was. But how are we supposed to climb out of him?

Eyre Do you know what a window is?

Judith Of course we do. Window is my moth—

Zilpah Oh, you nincompoops! A window is a structure that links a room to the outside. By climbing through it we may reach the outside.

Judith There he goes again, Jethro, shooting his mouth off about the outside. Outside this, outside that! What is a high society woman to do in the company of such a psychopath?

Jethro We could leave this room.

Judith Oh, Jethro! Do you think it's possible?

Jethro Yes, I do.

Judith Everybody! May I have your attention?! My Jethro has just come up with the most intelligent idea! We shall go outside!

Jethro I propose we go outside via one of the windows. Now everybody check the windows. By check—

Anon [*shouting*] Door!

Eyre What, Anon?

Anon [*quietly*] There's a door.

Eyre You mean—

Anon I've wanted to go out for a long time. I couldn't.

Eyre Why?

Anon She stopped me.

Eyre Who?

Magnus Me.

Magnus rises from her chair.

I stopped him. Do you know what you have done to everybody in this room, child? You have put false dreams and illusions into their heads. You have promised them more than they can handle…

Eyre More…

> *The others who have been desperately clawing at the windows slowly begin to turn their heads towards Eyre.*

More ways to escape this room. You come too, Magnus?

Magnus You don't get it, do you, child? Outside is evil, corrupt and filled with things that appear in nightmares. [*Addressing the room*] My son went out once and he was left affected…

Judith Affected?

Jethro Affected.

Judith Unnatural.

Jethro Abnormal.

Judith Eccentric.

Jethro Weird.

Judith Stupid.

Jethro Dumb.

Judith [*lost for a word*] Oh dear…

Jethro [*whispering to her*] Mute.

Judith Thank you, darling. Mute.

Magnus Son, come here.

Anon walks slowly towards Magnus, followed by the stares of the room.

He has become mute because of the horrors he saw. Tell them, child; tell them what you saw…

Anon A glimpse.

Zilpah [*reaching for his notebook*] Wait, I must record…

Anon I recorded.

Zilpah You did?

Anon I recorded.

Zilpah Where? What?

Anon Pictures.

In the sudden excitement of making a scientific discovery, Zilpah lunges for Anon's pictures.

Zilpah These? Why they're extraordinary.

Anon Outside was beautiful.

Magnus No! He tells lies. You stupid, stupid child!

Anon I am still in awe of what I saw. That is why I *not* talk. For a moment I was happy.

Magnus No! You are happier here! Anon! You are happier here! You all are!

Zilpah [*ignoring Magnus*] You mean you saw beauty.

Anon A glimpse.

Zilpah Positively amazing. Why, beauty is something I have only read about in books.

Judith Beauty? It's something I find in jewellery.

Jethro In money.

Wilmah In the old days.

Eyre Outside.

A long pause as they reflect on what they consider to be beautiful.

Anon Here is the key to the door, Eyre.

Contemplative pause.

Magnus Traitors. All of you are traitors! How dare you backstab my room that I have graciously given you! I made you feel comfortable, happy—

Judith Trapped. [*Truthfully asking Eyre*] Eyre, do you think I will find happiness outside? More happiness than what money can buy?

Eyre I not know but *you* will never know unless open the door.

Magnus Fools! Don't believe her! You won't find what you're looking for outside! You will surely crumble.

Zilpah [*to Eyre*] Will I be able to apply my knowledge outside?

Eyre Apply, yes, and many opportunities to do so.

Magnus [*scornfully*] I won't be opening that door once you're gone, for any of you. You will be lost forever.

Wilmah Will there be colour and warmth and fun like I used to have in my childhood days?

Eyre I not know.

Magnus Uncertainty. Unknown. Undiscovered territory. Are you willing to risk your life for something that you don't even know exists?

Anon I saw it. I want to see it again. I want to go outside.

> *Eyre looks at the key. She walks towards the door and places the key in the lock. She turns the key and there is a distinct 'click'. The door is unlocked, but not yet open. Eyre walks back. Judith, followed by Jethro, approaches the door.*

Judith Jethro?

Jethro I'm right behind you, darling.

Judith Ready?

Jethro Yes.

Judith Darling, I… I… can't.

Jethro Neither can I.

Judith & Jethro [*together*] I'm afraid.

Magnus [*triumphantly*] Fear!

Judith I can't leave, we don't even know what is out there.

Jethro We'd be risking our lives.

Judith [*snapping back to her selfish self*] And not to mention my jewellery. Give me comfort and my Dumont pearls any day.

> *They abruptly storm away from the door, almost as though they are secretly afraid of it. Zilpah makes his way to the door.*

Zilpah It's time to venture into the unknown, like Gilgamesh of the ancient world. Farewell to this crazy bunch. I bid you goodbye, Judith, Jethro, Magnus, Anon, Wilmah, Eyre and my books. [*Alarmed*] My books! I can't leave them behind. They're my life source. I can take them, can't I?

Eyre Zilpah, you not need book, you have knowledge.

Zilpah Correct, 'knowledge is power'.

Magnus [*cockily*] Knowledge is nothing without references.

Zilpah [*sighing*] I can't leave. I only own books and without books there is no knowledge.

Magnus [*triumphantly*] Confusion.

Zilpah I can't. Perhaps another time when I have more knowledge. Or is it power? Or is it…?

> *Zilpah returns to his books. Wilmah approaches the door.*

Wilmah I can't.

Eyre You must to discover joy of childhood.

Wilmah No, I can't remember my childhood, dear. I've been in here so long. I can't remember the outside joy of my childhood. What if it isn't there? What if there are no such things as watermelons anymore? What if I turn to dust? What am I talking about?

Eyre [*feeble*] Come, please?

Wilmah I'm too old.

Magnus Limits!

Eyre What about your purpose? Fuvzat?

Wilmah I suspect he's dead. He died long ago when I came in here…

> *Wilmah touches the door and for a minute she is partly sane. She backs away and makes way for Anon.*

Magnus [*in a desperate plea*] No, son, I need you. You're mine. I only have you. Please stay.

Anon I cannot. I need to explore. You can no longer—

Magnus [*pure contempt*] Hold you back.

Anon This room is dark and my future is bleak. I need to discover. I need to—

Magnus [*hypnotic*] Stay. To keep your mother happy.

Anon I need to—

He reaches for the door handle.

Magnus [*powerfully*] Stay!

He has succumbed to his mother's trance. He lets go of the door handle. He retreats to her side. His expression is blank. There is a long pause. Eyre makes her way over to the door. She holds the door handle in a firm grip and turns to give her final thoughts.

Eyre If you stay in this room, I can tell you who, where and what you will be in a hundred years from now. You will be the same, except older. You will be here, except unhappier. You will be doing what you are doing now, wondering what it might have been like if only you had opened the door.

She opens the door and a brilliant light illuminates the room.

If you leave this room of comfort, I cannot predict your future. There is no limit to who you can be, where you can go and what you will do. The choice is yours, take it.

She drops the key. Eyre turns and leaves the room.

There is a stunned silence. Jethro is the first to move. He takes a record and places it in the gramophone. Judith, defeated, takes her husband's lead to dance. He tightly embraces her. It makes no difference. She is still lost in deep thought. The record starts to play 'The Blue Danube'. The music dies down.

Judith [*sullenly*] Jethro, darling, do you sometimes wonder what it would have been like if we had—?

Jethro [*interrupting*] Yes.

Judith Tell me again, why didn't we?

Jethro It was the unknown.

Judith Ah, the unfamiliar.

Jethro The unascertained.

Judith The undiscovered.

Jethro The unexplored.

Judith The uninvestigated.

Jethro The unrevealed.

Judith The un… un…

Jethro [*whispering in her ear*] Unearthed.

Judith Oh, thank you, darling. The unearthed.

They waltz a while.

Jethro The fact was we were—

Judith Don't say!

Jethro Scared.

Judith Frightened.

Jethro Alarmed.

47

Judith Worried.

Jethro Unsure.

Judith Terrified.

Jethro Apprehensive.

Judith We were… ah… oh…

Jethro [*whispering in her ear*] Afraid.

Judith Oh, thank you, darling. Afraid.

Jethro But we're comfortable, are we not?

Judith Why, yes. Yes! I suppose so.

Jethro And we're happy?

Judith [*uncertain*] Actually, now that I consider it—

Jethro [*concludingly*] No.

Judith No.

Jethro No? So you are happy.

Judith No. 'No' as in 'no, I'm not happy'.

Jethro Well, why don't you look at your jewellery?

Judith I… I… I don't think that's going to make me happy anymore. [*She suddenly stops waltzing.*] She made me realise that money can't buy certain things. Yes, it can buy sapphire rings and ruby necklaces but it can't buy—

Jethro Diamonds?

Judith [*longingly*] Freedom.

Jethro The ability to fly like a bird.

Judith Soar like an eagle.

Jethro To come down from the bleachers and onto the field.

Judith To… to…

Jethro [*whispering in her ear*] To cut the…

Judith Jethro, please, give me a chance. [*She pauses. Solemnly*] To walk out of the door.

Jethro [*unconvincingly*] Chin up, darling. There is always next time.

Judith Next time.

> *The record screeches. Everybody on stage freezes. Wilmah comes forward.*

Wilmah There was no next time. Eyre and the others like her never came back. Yes, there were others like Eyre who ventured outside. They mustn't have liked our room's décor because they never decided to come back. I never found Fuvzat but I expect Eyre found Luther. Zilpah went mad soon after Eyre left. He couldn't stop cramming all those silly books into his head. He even ate one! Judith and Jethro divorced. It's all hush-hush at the moment. Although I did hear that there was some talk of Jethro having an affair with a Fuzzwollop. Made for each other those two. Magnus doesn't talk much anymore. Not since… well… Anon died. He had a bad case of claustrophobia. In fact, nobody talks much anymore. I think everybody still wonders about Eyre and the outside and what it might have been like if we had taken the opportunity. Nothing stopped us from leaving, we all know that. We could've left but we were comfortable. It's a bad thing, comfort. You should never be comfortable! I found a key yesterday, when I was autumn cleaning. I might go outside. Just for a bit. It's never too late, you know.

The lone fluorescent light begins to blink.

I think everybody hangs on the last words Eyre said: 'The choice is yours, take it...' She was right, it's no fun being comfortable and life is just too short not to leave our frame of mind.

The light flickers off. There is the sound of a key turning a lock. A brilliant light illuminates the stage and then it fades to darkness.
Blackout.

THE END